FOREIGN TAXES AND THE GROWING SHARE OF U.S. MULTINATIONAL COMPANY INCOME ABROAD: PROFITS, NOT SALES, ARE BEING GLOBALIZED

Harry Grubert[1]

February 22, 2011

The foreign share of the worldwide income of U.S. multinational corporations (MNCs) has risen sharply in recent years. Data from a panel of 754 large MNCs indicate that the MNC foreign income share increased by 14 percentage points from 1996 to 2004. The differential between a company's U.S. and foreign effective tax rates exerts a significant effect on the share of its income abroad, largely through changes in foreign and domestic profit margins rather than a shift in sales. U.S.-foreign tax differentials are estimated to have raised the foreign share of MNC worldwide income by about 12 percentage points by 2004. Lower foreign effective tax rates had no significant effect on a company's domestic sales or on the growth of its worldwide pre-tax profits. Lower taxes on foreign income do not seem to promote "competitiveness."

Keywords: multinational corporations, domestic-foreign tax differentials, income shifting, foreign-source income

JEL Codes: F23, H25, H32

---

[1] I am grateful to Ralph Rector for providing me with very useful files and making helpful comments. Also, many thanks for helpful comments from Stephen Matthews, Douglas Shackelford, Geraldine Gerardi, two anonymous referees, and participants in seminars at the Oxford Centre for Business Taxation and the National Tax Association Annual Conference on Taxation. Additional comments can be sent to harry.grubert@treasury.gov. Nothing in this paper should be construed as reflecting the views or policy of the U.S. Department of the Treasury. This paper is forthcoming in the National Tax Journal.

I. INTRODUCTION AND SUMMARY

Since 1996 the share of the worldwide income of U.S. multinational companies (MNCs) that is declared abroad has increased significantly. This development has received a great deal of attention in the tax press (Sullivan, 2008), and is also reflected in the rather expansive estimates of the revenue that the United States would gain if it adopted formula apportionment (Avi-Yonah and Clausing, 2007).

Data from a linked sample of 754 large nonfinancial U.S.-based MNCs obtained from the Treasury corporate income tax files indicate that the share of aggregate pre-tax worldwide income earned abroad increased from 37.1 percent in 1996 to 51.1 percent in 2004.[1] This increase in the foreign share of total income was almost completely in the form of income that is not repatriated from abroad, which rose from 17.4 percent of worldwide income in 1996 to 31.4 percent in 2004. Foreign income here is defined as the equity income before foreign tax of the foreign subsidiaries of U.S. parent corporations. Domestic income is U.S. taxable income less dividends from abroad. It therefore includes royalties and interest received from foreign affiliates because they are deductible in the host country and included in the current U.S. tax base.

The objective of this paper is to use the firm level data to better understand the role of tax incentives in this dramatic change in the foreign share of worldwide MNC income. In particular, how would the foreign share of income be different if corporate foreign income were subject to accrual taxation at the normal 35 percent tax rate applied to domestic income? Tax differentials can provide incentives to increase investment abroad, and to shift income through transfer price manipulation, the location of company debt, and other mechanisms. These differences between

---

[1] As described in greater detail at the end of the paper, data published by the Bureau of Economic Analysis (BEA) of the U.S. Commerce Department show that foreign profits have continued to rise substantially as a percentage of total national profits since 2004.

domestic and foreign tax burdens have widened in part because of the greater opportunities for foreign tax planning made possible by several new regulations introduced in 1997.

After a brief review of recent papers that address some of these issues, the paper describes the data used in the empirical work, in particular how the foreign share of income and the average effective foreign tax rate are computed. These data are then used to estimate the effect that a company's average effective foreign tax rate has on its foreign share of worldwide income. Furthermore, because a company's foreign share of income can change either because of a change in the share of its worldwide sales abroad or in its foreign and domestic profit margins, these are also analyzed separately.

Various specifications and samples are used in the firm level analysis. One sample includes companies with worldwide losses in either 1996 or 2004, and the other sample excludes them so that foreign shares of worldwide income can be computed. Regressions are estimated for both the *change* in profit margins and sales and their *levels* in a given year. One series of regressions evaluates the role of intangible assets in facilitating income shifting. Another allows the sensitivity of foreign income shares and profit margins to tax differentials to change over time. The results consistently show that tax differentials have a significant impact on the foreign share of a company's worldwide income abroad, primarily through a change in profit margins rather than changes in the locations of sales. Furthermore the mobility of profits and sales in response to tax differentials seems to have increased over time.

An important question is the extent to which a decline in foreign tax rates affects the domestic economy. Does such a decline lead to a reduction in domestic sales or a decline in domestic profit margins? A fall in foreign tax rates can increase the share of worldwide income abroad but that may simply reflect greater sales and income abroad without implying any

2

reduction in U.S. domestic income. On conceptual grounds, foreign and domestic investment could be net substitutes or complements. In the firm level analysis, it is difficult to identify any significant positive or negative effect of lower effective foreign tax rates on domestic sales. Furthermore, lower foreign tax burdens have no impact on companies' worldwide profit growth from 1996–2004.

The paper then uses the firm level results to estimate the extent to which tax differentials contributed to the 14.0 percentage point increase in the foreign share of *aggregate* worldwide multinational income. It is first necessary to link the firm level evidence and the sample aggregates. The foreign share of aggregate MNC income can increase in two ways: because the companies with a high initial foreign income share grew faster worldwide than the average, or because the average company in terms of initial worldwide income increased its foreign income share over the period. Specifically, the change in the foreign share of aggregate worldwide MNC income can be expressed as the sum of two components: the change in each MNC's foreign share weighted by its initial 1996 share of worldwide income, and the change in each MNC's share of worldwide income weighted by its initial foreign share.

Each of the terms in these two components, including the weights, can be influenced by the foreign-domestic tax differential. For example, a large difference between a company's foreign and domestic effective tax rates in 1996 may have already raised its 1996 foreign share of income.

Because the various specifications and samples yield different quantitative estimates of the response of profit margins and sales to tax differentials, we present a range of estimates. A specification that allows for the tax sensitivity of sales and income to increase over time suggests that the combined effect of U.S.-foreign tax differentials in 1996 and the widening of those differentials from 1996 to 2004 increased the foreign share of total MNC worldwide income by about 12 percentage points.

Finally, because of the important changes in the U.S. tax treatment of foreign income after 1996, which are described in detail below, the paper attempts to identify the role they played in companies' ability to achieve greater reductions in their foreign effective tax rates. The introduction of the check-the-box provisions in 1997, which facilitated the shifting of income from high tax to low tax countries, seems to have accounted for 1 to 2 percentage points of the 5.0 percentage point decline in average foreign effective rates. The "active finance exception," which reinstituted deferral for income from active financial business abroad, accounts for about an additional 0.5 percentage point of this reduction.

We also include a section on qualifications and caveats because of limitations in the data and analysis that may bias the results. The final section summarizes the conclusions of the analysis.

II. RELATIONSHIP TO THE LITERATURE

The literature on the relationship between tax rates and the location of direct investment and income goes back at least to Grubert and Mutti (1991) and Hines and Rice (1994). The large number of subsequent studies is summarized recently in Organisation for Economic Co-operation and Development (OECD) (2008). Most of these studies are based on a cross section of host countries with varying tax rates. It is therefore impossible to determine whether high profit rates in a low tax location, such as Ireland, reflect income shifting from either corporations based in the United States or from their subsidiaries in high tax foreign countries. Similarly, there has been very little analysis of the effect of foreign-domestic tax differentials on increases or decreases of economic activity in the United States.

Two very recent papers are particularly relevant for the analysis in this paper. Clausing (2009) attempts to estimate the total amount of income shifted out of the United States using data published by the BEA. But, in contrast to the analysis here, the estimate is not based on the observed relationship between average foreign tax rates and domestic profit margins and sales. As in much of the income shifting literature, Clausing's statistical analysis is based on a cross-section of host countries for U.S. direct investment and the effective tax rates in those locations. After estimating the total income shifted to the low tax locations in the cross-section, Clausing then calculates how much of that is attributable to income shifted from the United States. This estimate is based on a comparison of how much subsidiaries trade with their parents and how much they trade with related parties in other foreign locations. Apart from being purely mechanical and somewhat arbitrary, this procedure ignores the fact that most income shifting from the United States is probably due to "non-transactions," i.e., subsidiaries paying inadequate royalties for U.S.-developed intellectual property.

Desai, Foley and Hines (2009) examine whether MNC investment abroad comes at the expense of investment at home. The direction of causation always arises as a problem when investigating this question because, for example, successful companies tend to expand everywhere. Furthermore, the relationship between foreign and domestic investment varies depending on the reason for the increased foreign investment. There could be various reasons, including the growth of foreign markets, lower costs abroad including taxes, or high trade barriers making exporting from the United States difficult. The authors address the causality issue by using host country GDP growth as an instrument for companies' foreign investment. They find that greater foreign investment is associated with greater domestic investment. But it is not surprising that GDP growth abroad results in greater MNC exports of U.S. components and headquarters services. However, the Desai, Foley and Hines findings have no bearing on whether an increase in U.S. taxes on foreign income would decrease domestic investment. Changes in foreign and domestic tax rates, or changes in any other relative cost variables, are not considered in their analysis.

In contrast, this paper uses foreign-domestic tax differentials to address the question of how taxes affect decisions by MNCs on where to locate investment and income. Using U.S. Department of the Treasury corporate tax files described in the next section, each MNC's average effective foreign tax rate is calculated, aggregating income and taxes paid across all its foreign subsidiaries. The resulting cross-sectional variation in companies' foreign-domestic tax differentials then identifies the extent to which lower foreign tax rates cause the shifting of income and economic activity in or out of the United Sates.

III. DESCRIPTION OF THE DATA AND EMPIRICAL STRATEGY

A. Data

A match of the 1996 and 2004 Treasury corporate tax files is the basis for identifying the sources of the increased share of MNC income abroad. These files include information from Form 1120 which is the basic corporate return, Form 1118 on which foreign tax credits are claimed, and Form 5471 which provides operating and balance sheet data for each of the company's controlled foreign corporations (CFCs). The total linked sample includes 754 nonfinancial corporations and 111 financial corporations. Most of the analysis concentrates on nonfinancial companies, which account for 88 percent of the foreign income in the sample in 2004. (A brief summary of the data on financial companies is contained in Appendix A.) The 865 companies we are able to link accounted for about 80 percent of total foreign MNC income in 2004.

The files are used to compute each MNC's average effective foreign tax rate in 1996 and 2004. Company foreign effective tax rates are computed from the total foreign taxes paid by subsidiaries in relation to pre-tax Earnings and Profits (E&P), a measure defined in the internal revenue code that approximates book income.[2] In summing subsidiary E&P we net out dividends that a subsidiary receives from a lower tier subsidiary to avoid double counting. As noted above, domestic income is defined as all pre-tax domestic taxable income reported on Form 1120, less dividends received from abroad. It therefore includes royalties and interest received from subsidiaries because they are included in the current U.S. tax base and deductible from host country tax abroad.[3] In contrast, foreign income can potentially be deferred.

We use the change in parent level average foreign effective tax rates rather than average statutory rates because the change in the effective foreign tax rate, i.e., total foreign taxes paid in relation to total pretax foreign income, can reflect the company's own tax planning efforts, such as shifting income from high tax countries to tax havens. This type of income shifting was greatly facilitated by regulations introduced in 1997. (These regulations are described in greater detail below in the analysis of the sources of the decline in effective foreign tax rates.) Prior to 1997, payments of interest and royalties from one subsidiary to another subsidiary would generally be subject to current U.S. tax under the anti-abuse CFC rules.[4] The 1997 regulations had the effect of allowing companies to defer this current U.S. tax until the funds were repatriated to the U.S. parent. Because of this newfound ability to shift income from one country to another, there may be little relation between where a subsidiary is incorporated and where its

---

[2] The effective foreign tax rates are computed from the company's CFCs that have positive profits. They may therefore not be a good measure of the company's long run incentives if there are large losses in other CFCs.
[3] Including repatriated dividends in domestic income as well was a possibility because they are also part of the domestic tax base. As indicated above, the increase in the share of worldwide income deferred abroad was virtually identical to the increase in the foreign share. But this would have necessitated an analysis of the repatriation decision, which is beyond the scope of this paper.
[4] The current tax does not apply if the income is subject to foreign tax greater than 90 percent of the top U.S. corporate rate.

income is located. It is therefore impossible to obtain weights for a composite measure based on country statutory tax rates. Accordingly, the average effective foreign tax rate is the best available indicator of the incentive to locate both economic activity and income abroad.[5]

On the domestic side, the U.S. statutory tax rate on corporate income remained at 35 percent from 1996 to 2004. As discussed in detail below, the changes in tax provisions over that period, such as those governing depreciation, were not large enough to have a significant effect on domestic effective tax rates. In any case, the 35 percent statutory rate is the most relevant rate for analyzing income shifting between the United States and foreign locations, as income that is shifted is taxed at the statutory rate. The average effective foreign tax rate is used on the foreign side because it is the best indicator of the relevant statutory rates.

The corporate tax files were used to construct basic company characteristics such as date of incorporation and total sales. Parent advertising expenses were taken from Form 1120. Research and development (R&D) expenditures were based on Qualified Research and Experimentation reported on the corporate return for the purposes of the Research and Experimentation (R&E) credit. This tends to be smaller than the amount of R&D stated on financial reports, in part because of rules specifying which expenditures qualify for the credit, and also because the R&E must be performed in the United States. In the small number of cases in which no credit is claimed but R&D is reported in Compustat, an imputation is made based on the Compustat entry.

In the empirical analysis, profit margins on sales are used as the profitability indicators and sales are used as the activity measure and investment proxy at home and abroad. The reason

---

[5] The country-by-country foreign income data published by the BEA in the U.S. Commerce department also does not reliably identify the country in which taxable income is located. As shown by Altshuler and Grubert (2005), a substantial fraction of the huge volume of inter-affiliate payments going to holding companies in tax havens is deductible in the country in which the income originates.

for the use of sales rather than assets or tangible capital is that the asset data in the Treasury files, and in particular the balance sheet on the parent's Schedule L, are unreliable. The main problem for the purposes of this paper is uncertainty about how foreign assets are included in total Schedule L assets. For example, some companies apparently report net equity in foreign subsidiaries and others include gross foreign assets on the asset side and foreign debt on the liability side. It is therefore difficult to calculate a valid measure of domestic assets. In contrast, the U.S. parent's own sales are given at the top of its Form 1120, and sales by each of its CFCs are reported on its Form 5471.

While reliable asset data might be preferred if available, the use of sales has some advantages. Unlike assets, sales are not subject to historical book value distortions. In addition, while self-developed intangible assets like patents and trademarks are usually carried at a zero basis on corporate balance sheets, their contributions to production are reflected in sales values, which is very useful since these assets play the critical role in cross-border investment.

B. Empirical Strategy

Companies can have different average effective foreign tax rates because they have different opportunities for the location of their activity. In other words, some companies' choice of location is more responsive to tax differences.[6] For example, mobile high tech companies that serve a worldwide market can easily locate in low tax jurisdictions. On the other hand, some companies find it more efficient to locate close to their customers, even if they reside in a high tax country.

Companies can also have lower foreign effective tax rates if they shift income from high to low tax countries. Firms that engage in more aggressive tax planning will have lower average

---

[6] For convenience, we sometimes refer to "foreign tax rates" and "average foreign tax rates," but in all cases "average effective foreign tax rates" is intended as the meaning.

effective foreign tax rates; that is, for a given difference in country tax rates, such firms will shift more income from the high tax country to the low tax country.

Greater sensitivity of investment location to local tax rates and more aggressive income shifting can create a relationship between observed average foreign tax rates and the foreign share of MNC income, either because a greater share of worldwide activity is located in low tax countries or because more of worldwide income is located there. Moreover, the location of investment and income reinforce each other. If a company invests in low tax locations, it has greater opportunities for shifting income there, further increasing the foreign share of income and lowering effective foreign tax rates. Aggressive tax planners lower foreign tax burdens, which in turn promotes more foreign investment.

We hope to identify this relationship between average effective foreign tax rates and the foreign share of income. Note that a relationship between average effective foreign tax rates and foreign profit margins would be observed only if there is income shifting from the United States. Shifting income from high tax foreign countries to low tax foreign countries would not affect pre-tax foreign or domestic profit margins, since such income remains within consolidated foreign income.

We use this observed relationship between effective foreign tax rates and foreign shares of income, and between foreign tax rates and domestic sales and profit margins, to estimate the impact of eliminating the tax incentives to invest and shift income abroad, for example, by eliminating the deferral privilege for active income abroad. Eliminating deferral would remove all tax incentives to locate income and activity in countries with tax rates below the rate in the United States, as all the factors that create the relationship between the foreign share of income and effective foreign tax rates would no longer be operative. The effects of differences in average foreign tax rates would disappear as all worldwide income would be currently subject to the U.S. tax rate. The companies that are in a position to take the greatest advantage of lower foreign tax rates under current law would have no more reason to shift income or locate activity abroad than those that cannot, or choose not to, take advantage of lower foreign rates. Even if the observed relationship between domestic profit margins and average foreign tax rates is due exclusively to different degrees of aggressiveness in income shifting to low tax countries, the estimated coefficient will reveal the impact of removing the opportunities for lower foreign rates. The profit margins of aggressive and non-aggressive MNCs would be similar.[7]

IV. THE IMPACT OF EFFECTIVE FOREIGN TAX RATES ON THE FOREIGN SHARE OF INCOME AND DOMESTIC AND FOREIGN PROFIT MARGINS

A. Different Samples and Specifications

The question to be investigated is the extent to which a lower effective foreign tax rate induces an increase in the share of a company's worldwide income abroad, and further how any increase is split between a shift in sales and a shift in profit margins. This will be identified mainly from the relationship between *changes* in foreign income shares, profit margins and sales on the one hand, and the *change* in effective foreign tax rates on the other. This has the advantage of controlling for unmeasured company characteristics that could bias the results. One specification includes the interaction of the parent's R&D intensity and the change in its effective foreign tax rate to examine the role of intellectual property in contributing to income shifting. In addition we also introduce a specification that permits the tax responsiveness parameters to change over time, for example, because of heightened capital mobility or more aggressive tax planning over time. It is therefore useful to look at a regression based on the levels

---

[7] The apparent endogeneity issues raised by the use of the observed relationship between the foreign share of an MNC's income and its effective foreign tax rate are discussed more fully at the end of the paper.

of the variables in 2004 to see if the results are consistent with the final transformed tax elasticities derived from this more flexible specification.

The regressions will be presented for two related samples. The first sample includes companies that may have worldwide losses in one or both of the two years analyzed. The only requirement is that companies reported foreign and domestic sales so that profit margins can be computed. (This requirement has virtually no impact on the aggregate change of the foreign share of income earned by the companies remaining in the sample, which is still 14.0 percentage points.) This sample contains 622 companies. The second sample, which excludes companies with worldwide losses in any of the two years so that foreign income shares can be computed, contains 415 parent-level observations.

In addition to the average effective foreign tax rate, the independent variables in the regressions include other possible determinants of the company's foreign income share. The ratio of parent R&D to sales and the ratio of advertising to sales are indicators of the levels of company intangible assets, which may increase the opportunities for profitable investment abroad. Regressions not displayed show that R&D and advertising have a statistically significant impact on worldwide profit margins.

Other independent variables are a dummy for companies incorporated after 1980 and a measure of the company's worldwide size in 1996. Less mature companies might be expected to have a smaller initial share of income abroad but their foreign share may rise more rapidly. Furthermore, large companies may have opportunities or handicaps different from smaller companies. (A table with the means of the variables used in the analysis is provided in Appendix B.)

In addition, the regressions for foreign and domestic profit margins include the worldwide profit margin as an independent variable. This variable measures the total pool of worldwide profits that can potentially be located either at home or abroad, while the effective foreign tax rate reflects the incentive for choosing one location rather than another. Apart from tax considerations, a company's profitability would be expected to be similar at home and abroad. The worldwide profit margin also controls for the possible correlation between worldwide profitability and effective foreign tax rates. Profitable high tech companies may tend be more mobile and locate in low tax countries. They may also have the opportunity for more aggressive tax planning. In fact, the negative correlation between effective foreign tax rates and worldwide profit margins is highly significant in 2004. R&D intensive companies obtained significantly greater reductions in effective foreign tax rates from 1996 to 2004. Excluding the worldwide profit margin as an explanatory variable in the profit margin equations could therefore result in serious omitted variable bias in the estimates of the tax coefficients.

B. Empirical Results

Table 1 presents the results of seven regressions estimating the changes in the shares of income, profit margins, and sales in response to changes in average effective foreign tax rates and other variables. The sample in Table 1 is limited to companies with positive worldwide profits in both years. The first regression shows that a change in a company's effective foreign tax rate has a large and statistically significant impact on its foreign share. The –0.436 coefficient, statistically significant at the 1 percent level, indicates that a 10 percent decline in the effective foreign tax rate would increase the foreign share of income by more than 4 percentage points.

Regressions 2 and 3 show that a reduction in effective foreign tax rates has a statistically significant effect on domestic and foreign profit margins. A lower foreign tax burden reduces the domestic profit margin while raising the foreign profit margin. Moreover the impact of a change in foreign effective tax rates is quantitatively significant. A 10 percentage point reduction in the effective foreign tax rate raises the foreign profit margin by 0.9 percentage points or about 10 percent of the 1996 mean. The domestic profit margin falls by almost as much, 0.75 percentage points. If income is shifted from the United States abroad because of the lower foreign tax rate, we would expect the foreign margin coefficient to be somewhat larger than the domestic margin coefficient in absolute value but opposite in sign, because domestic sales tend to be larger than foreign sales.

The statistically significant negative coefficient for company R&D intensity is noteworthy in the second regression. Domestic profit margins of high tech companies tended to decline from 1996 to 2004. The R&D variable has a positive coefficient in the foreign profit margin regressions but the estimates are not statistically significant. The role of R&D is examined further in Table 3 to see if it facilitates the shifting of income from the United States.

The relationship between the foreign share of income and foreign effective tax rates could in part be attributable to a shift in the composition of worldwide sales. But regressions 4 and 5 show that the change in the geographical composition of sales plays at most a minor role. In regression 4 for the change in the foreign share of worldwide sales, the change in the effective foreign tax rate is not statistically significant. In regression 5 where the change in the foreign share of sales is added as an explanatory variable in the change in foreign share of income regression, the sales share is statistically significant but the size and statistical significance of the change in foreign tax variable is not much affected (–0.370 compared to –0.436 in column 1). It is the effect of effective foreign tax rates on domestic and foreign profit margins that is important, not their effect on foreign and domestic sales.

We can also look at foreign and domestic sales separately to shed light on the longstanding controversy regarding the impact of foreign direct investment on the domestic economy. Is it the "export of jobs" view, as embodied in various legislative proposals to restrict "runaway plants," or the "foreign investment is good for America" view, as expressed by Desai, Foley, and Hines (2009), that turns out to be valid?[8] The answer to this question on the relationship between MNC foreign activity and the domestic economy depends on why foreign investment expands. Increased investment abroad because of growing foreign economies may have an effect on domestic output different from foreign investment increasing in response to lower effective foreign tax rates. Since the question is usually posed to guide U.S. tax policy, it is necessary to observe the actual domestic response to changing foreign tax burdens.

When examining the change in the log of domestic sales (regression 6), the change in the foreign tax rate coefficient is positive, indicating that a reduction in foreign tax rates reduces domestic sales, but the estimate is not statistically significant. The difficulty in identifying any significant positive or negative effect of lower foreign tax rates on domestic sales suggests that the positive effects, such as the increase in component exports to affiliates, offset the possible negative effect in the form of a shift in activity to foreign locations. Neither the "export of jobs to low tax locations" view nor the "low tax burdens on MNC income abroad increase domestic investment" view seems to have strong empirical support.[9]

---

[8] Sullivan (2010) presents anecdotal evidence in support of the "export of jobs" view based on the activity of a single company.

[9] The papers summarized in OECD (2008) indicate a significant impact of effective tax rates on the location of investment, but most of this evidence is based on the choice among foreign locations. The evidence on the choice between the home country and a foreign location is much weaker, particularly on whether the expansion abroad reduces expansion at home.

Regression 7 indicates that changes in the effective foreign tax rate also did not seem to have any statistically significant effect on foreign sales. As in the case of domestic sales, the tax coefficient is not statistically significant. One possible reason that lower foreign tax burdens do not have an effect on real activity is that companies can exploit lower tax rates by shifting income. Shifting investment and shifting income may be substitutes.

Looking at the size and post-1980-incorporation variables in the regressions presented in Table 1, we see that bigger companies tended to have larger increases in domestic profit margins and smaller increases in foreign profit margins. In both cases the size coefficients were statistically significant. Therefore, the foreign income shares of bigger companies increased less than smaller companies. Companies incorporated after 1980 had smaller increases in domestic profit margins and larger increases in foreign profit margins, although in this case the coefficients were generally not statistically significant.

Consistent with the firm level results for profit margins, the sample indicates that from 1996 to 2004 there was a major shift in domestic and foreign profit margins. The foreign (unweighted) mean profit margin increased by more than 5 percentage points, almost doubling, while the domestic margin declined by more than 3 percentage points (Appendix B, Table B1). Mean worldwide profit margins were virtually unchanged.

Table 2 replicates some of the analysis in Table 1 for the larger sample, which includes companies that had worldwide losses in one or both of the two sample years. The major difference is that in this case there can be no analysis of changes in the foreign income share. The results in the change of domestic and foreign profit margin regressions in the first two regressions are similar to those presented in Table 1. The changes in effective tax rate coefficients are each statistically significant at least at the 5 percent level, although they are somewhat smaller in absolute value than those presented in Table 1. It may be that the tax effects are smaller when companies with worldwide losses are included because decision making changes when there are worldwide losses. For example, if a company has a domestic loss and foreign profits, it would want to shift income back to the domestic operation to utilize the loss even if the foreign tax rate is much lower. Furthermore, the foreign effective tax rate measure is less meaningful if there are foreign losses. As described earlier, the measure we use is constructed from the CFCs that have positive income, but this may not give an accurate picture of the companies' long run incentives.

Previous work has suggested that the presence of intangibles greatly facilitates the shifting of income. For example, using data on subsidiaries in various foreign countries, Grubert (2003) finds that the shifting of intangible income and the allocation of debt explain almost all of the differences in profitability in response to taxes. Therefore, Table 3 presents profit margin regressions in which the interaction of the company's R&D intensity and the change in its average effective foreign tax rate is added as an independent variable; that is, this variable investigates whether R&D-intensive companies have a greater opportunity to exploit low foreign tax rates.

These results generally support the hypothesis that R&D-based intangibles facilitate income shifting. The first two regressions in Table 3 use the sample in Table 1 that was restricted to companies with positive worldwide income in both 1996 and 2004. The coefficient of the foreign tax rate-R&D interaction in the first regression has the expected positive sign but it is not statistically significant by normal standards. However, the coefficient of the change in foreign tax rate-R&D interaction term is highly statistically significant in the regression 2, which examines the change in the foreign profit margin. Furthermore, in regressions 2 and 3, which use the expanded sample including companies with worldwide losses, the coefficients for the change

in foreign tax-R&D interaction term are highly significant for both the domestic and foreign

profit margins. Intangible assets created by R&D permit companies to take greater advantage of

a relatively low foreign tax rate.[10] Since the intangibles are created in the United States, the

results confirm the findings in Tables 1 and 2 that lower foreign tax burdens increase the shifting

of income from the United States.[11]

As suggested at the beginning of the paper, companies can become more responsive over

time to a given tax differential, for example, by shifting income more aggressively. This can be

tested by adding the initial 1996 foreign tax rate to the change in foreign share regression.[12] The

regression results presented in Table 4 explore that possibility. The coefficient of the initial 1996

effective foreign tax rate is a measure of the increased responsiveness of shares and margins to

tax differentials. The coefficient of the change in the effective foreign tax rate becomes the final

responsiveness parameter after the change.

The first regression in Table 4, for the change in the foreign share, indicates that

companies indeed have become more responsive to tax differentials. The 1996 effective foreign

tax rate is statistically significant at the 5 percent level, indicating a substantial increase in

companies' sensitivity to tax differentials. Further, the coefficient of the basic change in the

effective foreign tax rate becomes much larger in absolute value and more statistically significant

---

[10] They may also help a company achieve a lower tax rate.

[11] As noted previously, the R&D used in this analysis is the amount that qualifies for the R&E credit and must be performed in the Unites States. In fact, R&D performed in the United States accounts for the overwhelming portion of company R&D. For example, Yorgason (2007) indicates that in 2004 U.S. parents performed 85 percent of total MNC R&D.

[12] This specification is suggested by starting with an equation in which the foreign share is a function of an elasticity parameter and the tax differential, and then taking the derivative of the foreign share with respect to time while allowing changes in both the tax differential and the elasticity. This can also be seen for discrete changes by subtracting a 1996 level equation from a 2004 equation, allowing the tax coefficients in each year to be different. This methodology was used in Altshuler, Grubert, and Newlon (2001).

compared to the Table 1 regression based on the same sample. This might be expected because it is the *final* tax response coefficient after the increased sensitivity to tax rates has taken place.

The remaining regression results displayed in Table 4 show that the greater sensitivity of the foreign share to the tax differential seems primarily attributable to changes in domestic profit margins and in the foreign share of worldwide sales. The second regression shows that the 1996 effective foreign tax rate had a significant impact on the change in domestic profit margins from 1996 to 2004. The coefficient is significant statistically at the 5 percent level with a positive sign as expected. In addition, the coefficient for the change in the effective foreign tax rate is much larger, almost twice the comparable coefficient in Table 1. But, surprisingly, the effective foreign tax rate in 1996 is not significant in the regression for the change in the foreign profit margin, although the coefficient of the change in the foreign tax rate variable is larger in absolute value than in the results presented in Table 1.[13]

The fourth regression in Table 4 shows that the tax sensitivity of the foreign share of sales also increased. The coefficient for the average effective foreign tax rate in 1996 is negative and statistically significant. The last two regressions indicate that this is attributable to the increase in foreign sales, not the decrease in domestic sales, although the effect does not seem very large.

This pattern of increased sensitivity to tax rates is also evident in comparable profit margin regressions, which are not displayed, that are based on the expanded sample in which companies with worldwide losses are included. The absolute size of the change in average effective tax rate coefficients in both the domestic and foreign profit margin regressions almost

---

[13] One possible explanation for the significant negative coefficient for the 1996 effective tax rate in the Table 4 regressions is the enactment in 2004 of the one-year tax holiday for dividend repatriations. In 2005, dividends could be repatriated at the low tentative U.S. tax rate of 5.25 percent compared to the normal 35 percent, with a proportionately scaled down foreign tax credit. Enactment of this provision became an active possibility as early as 2002. Firms therefore may have put a lower tax cost on income deferred in low tax locations abroad.

doubles. It therefore appears that the initial 1996 effective foreign tax rate is an important omitted variable in the earlier regressions presented in Tables 1–3, and that those results seriously underestimate the importance of tax differentials.

In contrast to the first four tables in which the 1996 to 2004 changes in the foreign share and profit margins are the dependent variables, Table 5 presents the results of regressions for the *level* of companies' foreign share and profit margins in 2004. As in Table 1, the sample is restricted to the companies that had positive worldwide income in both 1996 and 2004. Again the focus is on the impact of the company's effective foreign tax rate, which has a highly statistically significant impact on the company's foreign share of income, and its domestic and foreign profit margins. The tax coefficients tend to be much larger in absolute value than the comparable coefficients for the change in the effective foreign tax rate in the regressions presented in Table 1. The coefficients for the R&D-foreign tax rate interaction terms in regressions 4 and 5 for the domestic and foreign profit margins are also much larger and more significant. These quantitatively more significant responses to tax differentials in 2004 are consistent with the results in Table 4, indicating that the tax sensitivity of the foreign share of income and profit margins has increased over time. Indeed, the –0.914 effective foreign tax rate coefficient in the first regression in Table 5, for the foreign share of income, is similar to the –0.704 coefficient in Table 4 that represents the final tax sensitivity of the foreign share of income. (The tax effects in 2004 regressions using the sample that includes companies with worldwide losses, which are not displayed, are closer to those presented in Table 1.)

C. Summarizing the Range of the Tax Impacts

The results in Tables 1–5 can be used to estimate the impact of foreign-domestic effective tax differentials on the foreign share of MNC income. The regressions consistently indicate that a company's effective foreign tax rate has a significant impact on the foreign share of its worldwide income, and on its domestic and foreign profit margins in particular. The results also support the hypothesis that opportunities for tax-induced income shifting are strongly influenced by the presence of intangible assets. However, the size of the tax effect varies depending on the sample and the specification.

We can illustrate the range of possible impacts by starting with the initial 1996 tax differential. The highly significant –0.436 coefficient for the change in effective foreign tax rates in the results of the first regression presented in Table 1 indicates that the approximate 10 percentage point differential between foreign and domestic effective tax rates in 1996 raised the foreign share of MNC income by more than 4 percentage points by 1996.[14] Furthermore, the results of the last regression presented in Table 1 indicates that the tax coefficient only decreases to –0.370 when the change in foreign sales is added to the regression, showing that the tax impact is almost exclusively through changes in profit margins.

In the regression results presented in Table 2, which include companies with worldwide losses in one or both of the years in the sample, there is no foreign share equation but we can estimate the foreign share from the profit margin equations. The basic tax coefficients for the domestic and foreign profit margins are on average only about 55 percent in absolute value of those for the more restricted sample analyzed in Table 1. On the other hand, the R&D-tax change interaction term coefficients in Table 3 tend to be larger and more significant. But using instead the basic coefficients for the change in the effective foreign tax rate in Table 2, the estimate of the effect of the 10 percentage point tax differential on the 1996 foreign share would therefore be closer to 2.5 percentage points.

---

[14] Appendix Table B1 indicates an average effective foreign tax rate in 1996 of 21.3 percent. U.S. General Accountability Office (2008) provides estimates of domestic effective tax rates. When state corporate taxes are included, 10 percentage points may be an underestimate.

The coefficients presented in Table 4, which reflect the specification allowing the sensitivity of foreign shares to change over time, suggest a much larger impact — a 7 percentage point increase in the foreign share of income as a result of the 10 percentage point tax differential. The level regressions for 2004 presented in Table 5 indicate an even larger impact of taxes, with the 10 percentage point tax differential resulting in a 9 percentage point increase in the foreign share of income. The estimated effect of the 10 percentage point domestic-foreign tax differential in 1996 therefore covers a wide range, from 2.5 percentage points to 9 percentage points of worldwide income. Because of the generality of the specification that allows the tax responsiveness to change over time as income becomes more mobile, the 7 percentage point estimate is our preferred estimate.

V. COMPONENTS OF THE CHANGE IN THE FOREIGN SHARE AND THE ROLE OF TAXES

The firm level results can now be used to estimate the role of foreign-domestic tax differentials in the 14 percentage point jump in the foreign share of total MNC income. But in order to link the firm level data and the change in the foreign share of aggregate MNC income, it is useful to decompose the change in the aggregate share into its constituent parts.

A. The Decomposition

The initial aggregate foreign share of worldwide income, S, can be expressed as the sum of each MNC's foreign share weighted by its share of total worldwide income: $S = \sum_i s_i w_i$, where s is the individual MNC's foreign income share and w is the MNC's weight in worldwide income. Taking the derivative of the aggregate S with respect to time and gathering terms we find that

$$(1) \quad \frac{\partial S}{\partial t} = \sum_i w_i \frac{\partial S_i}{\partial t} + \sum_i s_i \frac{\partial w_i}{\partial t}.$$

The first summation term on the right hand side is the change in the individual MNC's foreign share weighted by the MNC's initial share of worldwide income, and the second summation is the change in each MNC's share of aggregate worldwide company income weighted by its initial foreign share. These are our basic components. However, in implementing this decomposition it is necessary to calculate companies' foreign share, which is impossible if worldwide income is negative. Therefore, companies with worldwide losses, either initially in 1996 or in 2004, are considered separately before proceeding with the full analysis based on the firm level data.[15]

B. Estimating the Components

1. Effect of Excluding Companies with Worldwide Losses

Implementing the above decomposition requires that worldwide income be greater than zero so that the share can be calculated. When companies with worldwide losses in either 1996 or 2004 are excluded from the sample, the growth in the aggregate foreign share of income falls from 14.0 percentage points to 11.3 percentage points. This 2.7 percentage point decline could have two basic sources. One is that some companies' domestic income declined so much from 1996 to 2004 that they resulted in a worldwide loss in 2004. Another is that companies with foreign losses large enough to cause a worldwide loss in 1996 had foreign income large enough in 2004 to eliminate the worldwide loss. But in regressions and probits to explain the occurrence of these patterns, the change in effective foreign tax rates did not seem to have any significance.

It is true that domestic losses seemed to become more important in 2004. Tabulations of the linked sample show domestic losses increased from 2.1 percent of worldwide income in 1996

---

[15] In the application below, the estimates use finite changes in shares and worldwide growth. There is therefore an interaction term that has to be assigned to one of the components. Since the component composed of company worldwide growth weighted by the initial share is calculated first, the interaction term is implicitly assigned to the second component.

to 5.8 percent of worldwide income in 2004. In contrast, there was only a modest increase in the significance of foreign losses, from 0.5 percent of worldwide income to 1.2 percent.

2. The First Component: Companies' Worldwide Income Growth Weighted by their Initial Foreign Share of Income

The first basic component is the increase in the aggregate foreign income share attributable to the growth of each company's worldwide profits from 1996–2004, holding its initial foreign share of income constant at its 1996 level, which is the second term in the decomposition equation above. This component provides the answer to a simple question: What would have happened to the aggregate share of foreign income if each company had maintained the same foreign share of worldwide income in 2004 as in 1996 but experienced its own actual change in worldwide income? The answer is that the foreign share of overall worldwide income in the sample would have increased by 5.0 percentage points, or about 44 percent of the actual 11.3 percentage point growth in the sample in which companies with worldwide losses in either 1996 or 2004 were excluded. The companies that already had a large foreign share in 1996 grew much faster.

The first set of regression results presented in Table 6 illustrates the strong positive relationship between worldwide profit growth from 1996 to 2004 and the initial 1996 foreign share of income. The dependent variable is worldwide income growth, the ratio of worldwide income in 2004 to worldwide income in 1996. To examine the relationship between worldwide profit growth and the 1996 foreign share, we add the same variables used in the earlier regressions to control for other possible determinants of the firm's growth, its R&D and advertising intensity, the dummy variable for companies incorporated after 1980, and a size variable in the form of the log of worldwide sales in 1996.

The only statistically significant independent variable in the first regression is the foreign share of worldwide income in 1996, which is significant at the 1 percent level. The R&D and post-1980 incorporation variables have the expected signs but only approach borderline significance.

While the firm level results suggest that tax differentials already had a significant impact on foreign and domestic profit margins by 1996, the impact of the initial 1996 tax differential only explains about 1 percentage point of the *increase* in the foreign share from 1996 to 2004. That estimate is based on using the estimated coefficient in the first regression presented in Table 1 to adjust each company's foreign income share in 1996 for the effect of its foreign effective tax rate compared to the U.S. effective tax rate, and then examining how this foreign share, which is undistorted by taxes, alters the impact of its worldwide growth on its overall foreign income share in 2004.

As indicated in the decomposition (1), this component is the product of the company's initial foreign share and its actual worldwide profit growth from 1996 to 2004. Therefore, one question in assessing the role of taxes in this component is whether low foreign tax burdens enabled companies to achieve faster worldwide growth. The last two regressions presented in Table 6 attempt to answer that question. The dependent variable is again worldwide income growth as in the first regression, but the 1996 average foreign tax rate is added as an explanatory variable in regression 2 and the change in the foreign tax rate from 1996–2004 is added in regression 3. In neither case are the tax coefficients statistically significant, even at the 10 percent level. Lower effective foreign tax rates do not seem to be important contributors to worldwide growth. The importance of low tax burdens on foreign income for U.S. worldwide "competitiveness" does not seem to have much empirical support.

3. The Second Component: The Change of Companies' Foreign Share of Income Weighted by Its

Initial Share of Worldwide Income

The remaining 6.3 percentage points of the 11.3 percentage points increase in the aggregate foreign income share rise is attributable to the second component, the change in companies' foreign share weighted by their share of worldwide income. The approximate 5 percentage point decline in foreign effective tax rates between 1996 and 2004 widened the foreign-domestic tax differential to 15 percentage points (Appendix B, Table B1). Therefore, in view of the above discussion of the range of possible effects of the initial 10 percentage point tax differential on the share of foreign income, it appears that the 5 percentage point decline in the average effective foreign tax rate added from 1.25 percentage points to 4.5 percentage points to the foreign share of worldwide income. Our preferred specification, where the impact of tax differentials can change over time, suggests the increase is 3.5 percentage points.

Finally, no contribution of tax rates is attributed to the other term in this component, the share of worldwide income weights, because the results in Table 6 indicate that low effective foreign tax rates do not contribute to worldwide growth.

4. Adding Up the Components

Using our preferred specification where the response to tax differentials can change over time, we conclude that the combined effect of the initial 10 percentage point tax differential and its 5 percentage point increase from 1996 to 2004 increased the foreign share of worldwide MNC income by about 12 percentage points. This 12 percentage point estimate is the sum of 7 percentage points attributable to the initial 10 percentage point tax differential, the 3.5 percentage points attributable to the additional 5 percentage point increase in the tax differential, and the 1 percentage point estimated for the first component in the decomposition. The complete range of estimates based on the various specifications and samples is 5 to 15 percentage points.

VI. THE SOURCES OF FALLING EFFECTIVE FOREIGN TAX RATES — THE ROLE OF NEW U.S. RULES

Table 7 goes on to evaluate the sources of the decline in effective foreign tax rates, in particular the new tax planning opportunities provided by the changes in the U.S. tax rules after 1996. Two of the new U.S. tax rules introduced after 1996 are especially significant. The first is the implementation of the "check-the-box" rules in 1997. Prior to 1997, a payment of interest or royalties by one CFC to another would trigger a current U.S. tax liability. With the check-the-box rules, the MNC could declare one of the CFCs to effectively be an unincorporated branch of the other. But the host government still regarded this CFC as a corporation and would therefore permit a deduction for the payment. The payment would however not be subject to current U.S. tax, because from the U.S. Treasury's point of view the transfer of funds would occur within one consolidated entity. By using such "hybrid" entities, which are treated as corporations by the host country but as branches by the United States, MNCs are able to shift income from high tax to low tax countries, significantly lowering their overall foreign tax burdens, without incurring current U.S. tax liability.

A recent report by the Joint Committee on Taxation of the U.S. Congress describes the various structures that companies use in exploiting these new rules (Joint Committee on Taxation, 2010). One way to shift income from high tax countries to low tax countries is to use intercompany loans issued by a tax haven finance subsidiary to a hybrid entity that is an affiliate in a high tax country. Another device is to use R&D cost sharing agreements to locate patents in a tax haven subsidiary. The tax haven entity "shares" in the costs of an R&D development project and is thus entitled to a share of any royalties from the resulting innovation. The tax

haven subsidiary then licenses the innovation to a hybrid entity in a high tax location in exchange

for deductible royalty payments. The hybrid structure of the affiliate in the high tax country

again makes it possible to avoid current U.S. tax on these inter-affiliate payments.[16] These

schemes lower the companies' average foreign tax rates, irrespective of where their real

operations were located, thereby encouraging greater shifting of income from the United States.

The second significant new tax rule enacted in 1997 is the extension of the deferral

privilege to active financial income. The Tax Reform Act of 1986 repealed deferral for financial

income on the grounds that it was impossible to distinguish passive from active financial income.

Financial income was therefore taxed by the United States on a current basis as earned. The 1997

restoration of deferral for active financial business abroad was the beginning of a series of

temporary extensions of the active finance exception. The provisions specified the requirements

for financial income to be considered active.

Companies may differ in the extent to which they benefit from these new planning

devices because their situations differ. For example, companies with large operations in high tax

locations might have a greater incentive to use hybrid structures to shift income to tax havens. In

contrast, mobile high tech companies may already enjoy low average foreign tax burdens so that

the use of hybrid entities would provide smaller benefits. Therefore, in the analysis below, one of

the explanatory variables for the *change* in average foreign tax rates after 1996 is the average

foreign tax rate, because it would reflects the incentive for companies to exploit the new

---

[16] The use of check-the box to lower foreign tax burdens may have encouraged greater income shifting from the United States. But we should note that some of the new planning strategies can make foreign income "disappear." In this case, the entity is owned directly by the U.S. parent that extends it a loan. The entity is recognized as a corporation in the foreign jurisdiction but it is a disregarded entity from the U.S. point of view. Therefore any interest payments to the parent have no U.S. tax consequences because it is a payment within the consolidated domestic company. But if the foreign jurisdiction allows tax consolidation of related companies, the interest deduction abroad can be used to offset the income earned by other operating companies in the same country. This strategy could cause the increase in the share of foreign income to be understated.

planning devices.[17] Furthermore, the check-the-box variable described in the next paragraph is measured with error, so the initial effective foreign tax rate may provide independent information. The incentive to lower foreign tax burdens would have been particularly strong if companies had a high initial foreign profit margin. Presumably the location of their real activities would have resulted in the high initial foreign tax rate. The introduction of the check-the-box regulations in 1997 implied that average foreign effective tax rates were no longer necessarily dependent on where companies' real operations were located.[18]

The expected effect of parent R&D intensity on the use of the new planning opportunities is ambiguous. Because of the difficulty in valuing high tech patents and products, intangible assets derived from R&D are important vehicles for income shifting (Grubert, 2003). Therefore low R&D intensity companies without the ability to shift intangible income may have found check-the-box particularly useful. (This effect could of course be reflected in a high initial foreign tax rate.) On the other hand, the new check-the-box rules made it possible for R&D-intensive companies to enter into a favorable cost sharing agreement with a tax haven subsidiary that would then receive royalties from operating hybrid affiliates in high tax countries.

Two new independent variables attempt to evaluate the significance of check-the-box and the active finance exception. The first is a measure of the use of hybrid entities. Form 5471 asks whether the subsidiary owns an entity that was "disregarded" under the check-the-box rules. A parent level check-the-box variable was constructed by giving a CFC a score of one if it reports a hybrid entity and zero otherwise, and then weighting the responses by subsidiary income.

---

[17] Note that this is distinct from the analysis of domestic and profit margins in 1996, for example, in which the level of the 1996 average foreign tax rate is an explanatory variable. In that case, having a lower average foreign tax rate is hypothesized to increase the incentive to shift income from the United States.

[18] The initial average foreign effective tax rate in the change in tax rate regressions also corrects for the simple noise in effective rates from year to year, as a transitory high rate in one year would be expected to be followed by a lower rate in the subsequent year.

The second new variable attempts to measure the extent to which a company might have benefited from the active finance exception. The tax files report the amount of financial services income that the parent company received from abroad in 1996. (Before 2007 repatriated financial services income was put in a separate basket for the purposes of computing credits for foreign tax on the income.) This is used to construct a Financial Services dummy variable that takes a value of one if financial services income was positive.

The other independent variables in Table 7 are the same as used earlier, the R&D and advertising intensity of the parent, a dummy variable for incorporation since 1980, and the size variable which is the log of company sales in 1996. R&D may play a role through companies' incentives to use hybrid entities and cost sharing agreements to shift income from high tax countries. Mature, larger companies may be in a better position to take advantage of the new planning opportunities.

Note that in Table 7 we regress the *change* in the average foreign tax rate on the *level* of the profit margin in 1996 on the grounds that companies with high foreign profit margins in 1996 had a greater incentive to use the new income shifting opportunities like check-the-box. This contrasts with the regressions in Table 5 where the *level* of the 2004 profit margin is regressed on the 2004 average foreign tax rate, and the regressions in Tables 1 and 2 where the *changes* in the profit margins are regressed on the *changes* in the foreign tax rate.

In the first regression in Table 7, the change in the average foreign rate from 1996 to 2004 is the dependent variable. The use of hybrid entities variable, which reflects whether the company takes advantage of the check-the-box rules, is significant at the 5 percent level and negative. As expected, companies use hybrid entities to lower their effective foreign tax rates. Parent R&D intensity also has a negative coefficient that is also significant at the 5 percent level,

30

consistent with the use of R&D cost sharing agreements and hybrid entities to lower foreign tax burdens. As expected, the initial effective foreign tax rate is highly significant statistically, and the initial foreign profit margin is significant at the 5 percent level.

The second regression is for the check-the-box variable itself, that is, the extent to which a company uses hybrid entities. The explanatory variables are again the company's R&D and advertising intensity, the corporate age indicator, the financial services dummy, the foreign effective tax rate in 1996, as well as the company's size and its foreign share in 1996. R&D-intensive companies would be expected to use hybrid entities to strip royalties from high tax countries. Companies with a high initial foreign share and a high initial foreign tax rate would have a greater incentive to lower foreign taxes. Larger companies would be in a better position to incur the costs of new tax planning.

Note the difference in the causation sequences between the first and second regressions. In the first regression, the hypothesis is that the *change* in the effective foreign tax rate depends on the intensity of the use of hybrid entities among other variables. In the second regression, the hypothesis is that the use of hybrid entities depended on the *initial levels* of the foreign tax rate and the foreign share of income.

The R&D intensity of the parent is highly significant statistically at the 1 percent level. The foreign share of income in 1996, which reflects both the relative size of foreign operations and their profitability in 1996, is also highly statistically significant. Surprisingly, the foreign tax rate in 1996 is completely insignificant in explaining companies' use of check-the-box, as a high foreign tax rate might be expected to result in a greater use of hybrids. Finally, the size of the company in 1996 is statistically significant in increasing the use of check-the-box. Large companies were in a better position to take advantage of the new planning opportunities.

The results of the third regression presented in Table 7 again have the change in the effective foreign tax rate as the dependent variable as in the first regression, but add two independent variables, the interaction of the 1996 effective foreign tax rate with the hybrid entity variable, and the interaction of the parent's R&D intensity with the hybrid entity variable. Both coefficients are highly significant, one at the 5 percent level and the other at much more than the 1 percent level. Check-the-box had a significant effect, particularly in R&D-intensive companies and those with high initial foreign tax burdens. Even though companies in high tax countries did not make more intensive use of hybrid entities than those in low tax locations, the ones in high tax locations benefitted much more from their use.

The financial services dummy has a negative coefficient but in the first regression it fails to be significant even at the 10 percent level. In the last regression, with the interaction variables, it just misses being significant at the 5 percent level. These results suggest that the active finance exception may have had an effect in inducing companies to lower their foreign tax burdens.

The hybrid entity coefficient in the first regression, which is combined with the mean of the variable (0.255 from Table B1) to get the mean effect, suggests that hybrid entities "contributed" more than 1 percentage point of the approximate 5 percentage point decline in average effective foreign tax rates. Using instead the coefficients in the third regression presented in Table 7, which include the interaction terms, the use of hybrid entities is estimated to have contributed more than 2 percentage points to the decline in effective tax rates. This range of estimates is roughly consistent with Altshuler and Grubert (2005), who estimate that U.S. companies used check-the-box to lower their foreign tax burden annually by approximately $7.0 billion by 2002. Similarly, the coefficient for the financial services variable, combined with the frequency of the dummy, suggests that the active finance exception may have contributed about 0.5 a percentage point of the decline.

VII. QUALIFICATIONS AND CAVEATS

A. Possible Endogeneity Issues

The relationship between foreign income shares and average effective foreign tax rates is not a "normal" type of relationship in which the tax rate is purely exogenous to the firm. The relationship reflects companies' own decisions, with more aggressive, more mobile firms having both a lower tax rate and a greater foreign share of income. For example, a more aggressive company will shift more domestic income to low tax countries, simultaneously changing both the average effective foreign tax rate and the foreign share. Nevertheless, we can use the observed relationship to project what would happen if the tax burden on foreign income were set at the U.S. rate. In that case, the aggressive, mobile firms would have no more incentive to move either sales or profits to low tax locations than less mobile and aggressive firms.

It is possible to argue that a company which for some reason has a high profit margin abroad has a greater incentive to lower its foreign tax rate, so the direction of causation goes from foreign margins to foreign tax rates. In fact, there is some evidence for this when, in Table 7, we relate the *change* in foreign effective tax rates to the *initial* foreign profit margin because of the special income shifting opportunities offered by new features of the U.S. system. Companies with greater initial foreign profits had a greater incentive to exploit the new planning opportunities in order to lower their foreign tax liabilities.

But the test of whether the causation from foreign shares to foreign tax rates is important in interpreting our results can be found in what happens to domestic profit margins. If higher initial foreign profits motivate a company to simply arrange a lower foreign tax rate, this should have no necessary implications for its domestic profit margins. In fact, the company might be expected to have high domestic profit margins as well because it is relatively profitable on a worldwide basis. Therefore, if a lower average foreign tax rate is associated with *both* a higher foreign profit margin and a lower domestic profit margin, which is what we find, it would suggest that income is being shifted out of the United States in response to the ability to achieve lower foreign tax burdens.[19]

Similarly, a company that needed to be near foreign customers might choose the low tax locations in the neighborhood. For example, a company that wanted a European base might choose to locate in low tax Ireland. Again, what happens to domestic profit margins compared to sales indicates the importance of this possibility. As we have seen, the relationship between changing foreign share and changing effective foreign tax rates is mainly attributable to a shift in domestic and foreign profit margins, not a shift in the location of sales.

Furthermore, the results on the role of R&D based intellectual property confirm the relationship between effective foreign tax rates and income shifting. The presence of parent-developed intellectual property both enables companies to achieve lower effective foreign tax rates and in turn magnifies the impact of tax differentials because it is so difficult to value accurately.

Another endogeneity issue is raised by the inclusion of the worldwide profit margin as an independent variable in the profit margin regressions. A shock to the foreign profit margin, for example, is transmitted to the worldwide profit margin. The coefficient for the worldwide profit margin may therefore be biased. But the effective foreign tax rate is the principle variable of interest and the worldwide profit margin was included to avoid omitted variable bias in its

---

[19] The shifting itself would not necessarily further lower average effective foreign tax rates. The income could just be shifted proportionately to the country in which the income contributed to the new lower average rate.

coefficients. High tech companies tend to be very profitable on a worldwide basis and have lower effective tax rates. The specification embodies the relatively straightforward hypothesis that an MNC's foreign and domestic profit margins would be similar apart from tax considerations.

B. Possible Biases in the Estimated Foreign Share

As indicated above, the measure of foreign income is "earnings and profits" (E&P), which is defined in the Internal Revenue Code and approximates book income. E&P is measured using specific asset class lives and straight line depreciation, and other adjustments that distinguish it from domestic or foreign taxable income. Domestic income is U.S. taxable income, which can be affected by changes in depreciation and other changes in the measure of taxable income. It is therefore necessary to address the possible bias introduced by the somewhat different measures we use for domestic and foreign income. The definition of E&P was unchanged in the period covered by this paper. The question is the importance of changes that affected the measurement of domestic taxable income after 1996.

The most important was "bonus depreciation," a temporary provision that was introduced in 2002 and expanded in 2004. Firms could take an additional first year depreciation deduction of 30 percent (50 percent after 2004) of the adjusted cost basis of certain assets. The basis for depreciation was reduced in later years to reflect the larger initial deduction. Altshuler et al. (2009) show that bonus depreciation had a substantial effect, reducing aggregate corporate taxable income by about 10 percent in 2004.[20]

However, bonus depreciation seems to have been less important in our linked sample of large MNCs for which intangible assets created by R&D and advertising are very significant. In fact, in this sample, depreciation declined from 5.18 percent of domestic sales in 1996 to 4.45

---

[20] I am grateful to Matthew Knittel for providing me with the adjustments used in their paper.

percent of sales in 2004. It also declined in relation to gross profits after cost of goods sold and in relation to EBITDA (earnings before interest, tax, depreciation, and amortization).[21]

Another possible source of bias in the use of taxable income as a measure of domestic income is the growing use of stock options as a component of corporate compensation. The gain on "nonqualified" options, which were the most important type of option issued during this period, is deductible from corporate income when exercised. Such options may simply be a substitute for wages but, at a minimum, the timing of deductions can be distorted. But the Altshuler et al. data indicate that the net effect of these deductions peaked in 2000 and was much smaller in absolute terms in 2004 than in 1997, the first year in their analysis. Stock options are very unlikely create problems of understating 2004 taxable income, relative to income in 1996.

The American Jobs Creation Act of 2004 introduced the 9 percent deduction for the income derived from domestic production activities, but this provision was not effective until 2005. It was intended as a replacement of the Extra-Territorial Income (ETI) provisions that had replaced the Foreign Sales Corporation (FSC) rules in 2000. The change from FSC to ETI may have some effect on the 2004 to 1996 comparison because it moved the dividends received deduction into the category of "other deductions." Our measure of domestic taxable income is before deductions for dividends received. But this factor seems relatively minor. Total dividends received deductions in 1996 in our sample were only 1.5 percent of net domestic income in 1996 and only declined slightly to 1.25 percent of income in 2004.

Therefore, any adjustment for the asymmetry between the measures of foreign and domestic income seems unnecessary. Any reduction in domestic taxable income relative to book

---

[21] Statistics of Income data indicate that aggregate corporate depreciation expense was essentially flat as a percentage of sales from 1996 to 2004 (Internal Revenue Service, Statistics of Income (1999) and (2007)). Depreciation expense in any year depends on industry mix and the pace of recent investment. The fact that total depreciation expense was flat as a percentage of sales in spite of bonus depreciation suggests that investment in tangible property was declining.

income would of course represent a reduction in effective domestic tax rates. The impact of domestic-foreign effective tax rate differentials would therefore be understated. In any case the U.S. statutory rate remained constant at 35 percent and that is the key factor creating incentives for income shifting, which turns out to be the most important consequence of tax differentials.

Finally, there may be some suspicion that changes in exchange rates, in particular the fall in the dollar, explain a part of the increase in the foreign share of income. But the trade-weighted indices published by the Federal Reserve Board of Governors indicate that, if anything, the opposite is true for the period between 1996 and 2004.[22] For example, the Broad Index for the nominal value of the dollar increased from 97.46 to 113.76 and the real value increased from 88.52 to 99.01.

C. Other Caveats

There are several factors causing our estimated impact of average effective foreign tax rates to be biased downward. One is the likely error in the measure of average effective tax rates. As described above, it is based on the taxes paid by subsidiaries with positive foreign income. Even if there are no subsidiaries with losses, effective tax rates can vary substantially from year to year because of the timing of deductions and credits. Similarly, the measures of the use of hybrid entities and of the importance of an MNC's financial operations are necessarily crude and probably lead to underestimates of their role in the decline in effective foreign tax rates.

There may also be some bias in the estimates because the tax returns of all of companies with foreign income in 2004 could not be linked with their tax returns in 1996. As indicated earlier, this leaves almost 20 percent of 2004 foreign income out of the analysis. One major reason for the failure to link returns is that the taxpayers are too small to be sampled with certainty in any year. The entire group of companies with foreign income had average domestic

---

[22] http://www.federalreserve.gov/Releases/H10/Summary/default.htm.

sales about one sixth of the average sales in the matched sample. Not surprisingly, the foreign income share of the companies not linked is smaller than the linked sample, by about 10 percentage points. But their R&D intensity, measured as the ratio of parent R&D to domestic sales, seems comparable, so their response to tax differentials may be similar to the linked group.

There may be other reasons why some companies could not be linked. Their identification numbers could have changed because of a reincorporation or merger. Some companies may have become multinationals between 1996 and 2004. On the other hand, some companies may have dropped out because they were acquired by foreign companies. Foreign and domestic tax considerations may have played a role in these changes.

In interpreting the estimate above of the amount of MNC income shifted abroad, it is necessary to consider the possibility that a major regime change such as current taxation of foreign income at the 35 percent rate could induce takeovers by foreign companies. The preferred estimate of 12 percent of worldwide MNC income shifted abroad assumes that the universe of U.S. MNCs remains the same.[23]

Finally, this paper only focuses on the sales and profits of U.S. based MNCs at home and abroad. It does not address income shifting by foreign-based MNCs with operations in the United States. The data include the operations of U.S.-based companies in Puerto Rico if they are organized as CFCs incorporated in Puerto Rico. By 2004, most of the U.S. companies in Puerto Rico that had taken advantage of the Possessions Credit, which ended in 2005, had either converted to CFC status or ceased operations in Puerto Rico. The Puerto Rican operations are therefore included in the analysis of profit margins, etc., based on 2004 levels. However, the

---

[23] Simple expatriation or "inversions" of U.S. companies without a change in ownership or business has been severely restricted by the American Jobs Creation Act enacted in 2004.

conversion from their previous status may contribute some bias to the data on changes between 1996 and 2004.[24]

VIII. SUMMARY AND CONCLUSIONS

This paper examines recent changes in the foreign shares of worldwide income of U.S. MNCs, and arrives at the following conclusions.

1. Various specifications and samples consistently show that the differential between domestic and foreign effective tax rates has a significant effect on the share of MNC income abroad. This effect operates mainly through changes in foreign and domestic profit margins rather than changes in the location of sales. Companies with lower effective foreign tax rates have both higher foreign profit margins and lower domestic profit margins. This evidence of income shifting from the United States is supplemented by the finding that increased R&D performed in the United States magnifies the impact of U.S.-foreign tax differentials. The problems in pricing intellectual property thus create greater opportunities for income shifting.

2. The responsiveness to tax differentials of the locations of both income and sales has increased over time.

3. The estimates of the quantitative impact of tax differentials on the overall foreign share of MNC income vary depending on the sample and the specification. Therefore the estimates of the combined effect of the initial tax differential in 1996 and further increases from 1996 to 2004 cover a wide range, from about 5 percentage points of worldwide income to about 15 percentage points. The estimate based on the specification that introduces the possibility that the response to tax differentials has changed over time results in an estimated increase of about 12 percentage points.

---

[24] The Possessions companies receiving the credit were incorporated in the United States.

4. The check the box rules enacted in 1997, which facilitated the shifting of income from high tax to low tax foreign countries, seem to have contributed about 1 to 2 percentage points of the approximate 5 percentage point decline in foreign effective tax rates.

The paper also examined the relationship between a company's effective foreign tax rate and its domestic and worldwide growth, and reached the following conclusions.

5. It is difficult to detect any significant effect of lower foreign tax rates on domestic sales. The positive effects implied by the "low tax burdens on foreign income are good for domestic investment" argument and the negative effects implied by the "export of jobs" argument seem to cancel.

6. Lower tax burdens on foreign MNC income do not seem to increase companies' worldwide growth. The evidence for the "competitiveness" benefits of lower taxes on foreign income does not seem very strong.

Finally, the increase in the foreign share of the income earned by MNCs seems likely to continue to be an important issue. Data published by the BEA on foreign profits relative to total national profits, including both the profits of MNCs and purely domestic companies, suggest that the trend has continued and indeed may have accelerated after 2004. Using these data, Hodge (2011) shows that foreign profits were 26.3 percent of total national profits in 2004 and increased to 38.2 percent of total national profits in 2009.

REFERENCES

Altshuler, Rosanne, Alan J. Auerbach, Michael Cooper, and Matthew Knittel, 2009. "Understanding U.S. Corporate Tax Losses." In Brown, Jeffrey R., and James M. Poterba (eds.), *Tax Policy and the Economy 23*, 73–122. University of Chicago Press, Chicago, IL.

Altshuler, Rosanne, Harry Grubert, and T. Scott Newlon, 2001. "Has U.S. Investment Abroad Become More Sensitive to Tax Rates?" In Hines, James R., Jr. (ed.), *International Taxation and Multinational Activity*, 9–32. University of Chicago Press, Chicago, IL.

Altshuler, Rosanne, and Harry Grubert, 2005. "The Three Parties in the Race to the Bottom: Host Countries, Home Countries and Multinational Corporations." *Florida Tax Review* 7 (3), 137–209.

Avi-Yonah, Reuven, and Kimberly A. Clausing, 2007. "Reforming Corporate Taxation in a Global Economy: A Proposal to Adopt Formulary Apportionment." Hamilton Project Discussion Paper. Brookings Institution, Washington, DC.

Clausing, Kimberly A., 2009. "Multinational Firm Tax Avoidance and Tax Policy." *National Tax Journal* 62 (4), 703–725.

Desai, Mihir A., C. Fritz Foley, and James R. Hines Jr., 2009. "Domestic Effects of the Foreign Activities of U.S. Multinationals." *American Economic Journal: Economic Policy* 1 (1), 181–203.

Grubert, Harry, 2003. "Intangible Income, Intercompany Transactions, Income Shifting, and the Choice of Location." *National Tax Journal* 56 (1), 221–242.

Grubert, Harry, and John Mutti, 1991. "Taxes, Tariffs, and Transfer Pricing in Multinational Corporate Decision Making." *Review of Economics and Statistics* 73 (2), 285–293.

Hines, James R. Jr., and Eric M. Rice, 1994. "Fiscal Paradise: Foreign Tax Havens and American Business." *Quarterly Journal of Economics* 109 (1), 149–182.

Hodge, Andrew W., 2011. "Comparing NIPA Profits with S&P 500 Profits." *Survey of Current Business* 91 (3), 22–27.

Internal Revenue Service, Statistics of Income, (1999). *1996 Corporation Income Tax Returns.* Washington, DC.

Internal Revenue Service, Statistics of Income, (2007). *2004 Corporation Income Tax Returns.* Washington, DC.

Joint Committee on Taxation, 2010. "Present Law and Background Related to Possible Income Shifting and Transfer Pricing." JCX-37-10. Joint Committee on Taxation, Washington, DC.

Organisation for Economic Co-operation and Development, 2008. *Tax Effects on Foreign Direct Investment: Recent Evidence and Policy Analysis.* Tax Policy Study No. 17. Organisation for Economic Co-operation and Development, Paris, France.

Sullivan, Martin A., 2008. "U.S. Multinationals Shifting Profits Out of the United States." *Tax Notes* (March 10), 1078–1082.

Sullivan, Martin, 2010. "Medtronic Moves Jobs, Profits Out of U.S." *Tax Notes* (August 16), 687–693.

U.S. General Accountability Office, 2008. *U.S. Multinational Corporations: Effective Tax Rates Are Correlated with Where Income is Reported.* GAO-08-950. General Accountability Office, Washington, D.C.

Yorgason, Daniel R., 2007. "Research and Development Activities of U.S. Multinational Companies." *Survey of Current Business* 87 (3), 22–39.

APPENDIX A: FINANCIAL COMPANIES

Financial companies account for 12 percent of the foreign income in the sample in 2004. Their total foreign income increased from 16.78 percent of worldwide income in 1996 to 25.03 in 2004. Income deferred abroad increased from 9.94 percent of worldwide income in 1996 to 17.61 percent of worldwide income in 2004. While the financial companies as a whole are less globalized, at least in terms of the location of income, the increase in their income and deferrals abroad was similar to that of nonfinancial MNCs. In addition, their average foreign tax rate declined by about the same 5 percentage points.

However, the growth of domestic losses was not important in the case of financial companies, amounting to less than 1 percent of worldwide income in 2004. On the other hand, the financial companies that initially were the most globalized tended to grow the fastest. That seems to explain almost half of the increase in the foreign share of financial companies' worldwide income. Perhaps the companies that were already highly globalized were the ones that could most benefit from the new deferral opportunities offered by the active finance exception.

Table 1
Changes in Foreign Share, Profit Margins, and Sales (1996–2004)

	Dependent Variables						
Independent Variables	Change in Foreign Share of Income (1)	Change in Domestic Profit Margin (2)	Change in Foreign Profit Margin (3)	Change in Foreign Share of Total Sales (4)	Change in Foreign Share of Income (5)	Change in Log of Domestic Sales (6)	Change in Log of Foreign Sales (7)
Change in average effective foreign tax rate	−0.436*** (0.136)	0.075*** (0.029)	−0.090** (0.045)	−0.0736 (0.0492)	−0.370*** (0.135)	0.173 (0.226)	0.334 (0.420)
Parent R&D/sales, 2004	0.875 (1.71)	−0.641** (0.268)	0.555 (0.503)	0.440 (0.616)	−0.277 (1.27)	4.65 (2.83)	2.69 (5.27)
Parent advertising/sales, 2004	−1.10* (0.62)	0.307** (0.148)	0.046 (0.185)	−0.394* (0.225)	−1.50** (0.690)	−0.221 (1.03)	−2.34 (1.92)
Incorporation after 1980	−0.101* (0.052)	−0.0048 (0.0108)	0.0164 (0.0152)	0.004 (0.019)	−0.113** (0.051)	0.73 (0.085)	0.091 (0.159)
Size: log of sales 1996	−0.071*** (.019)	0.0157*** (0.0039)	−0.0147*** (0.0055)	−0.0129* (0.0067)	−0.062*** (0.018)	−0.048 (0.031)	−0.094 (0.058)
Change in worldwide profit margin		0.721*** (0.062)	0.533*** (0.088)				
Change in foreign share of sales					0.565*** (0.136)		

Notes: Robust standard errors are in parentheses. The number of observations is $N = 415$. The sample is limited to nonfinancial parent companies with positive worldwide income in both years. The change in the average foreign tax rate is the foreign effective tax rate in 2004 minus the foreign effective tax rate in 1996. The mean change is negative. Similarly, the change in the foreign share is the foreign share in 2004 minus the foreign share in 1996. The R&D and advertising variables refer to parent level R&D and advertising expenditures relative to domestic sales. The incorporation dummy variable is an indication of recently established companies. The log of worldwide sales is a measure of corporate size. The profit margins are the ratio of net income to sale

Asterisks denote significance at the 1% (***), 5% (**), and 10% (*) levels.

44

Table 2

Changes in Profit Margins and Sales
(1996–2004)

Independent Variables	Dependent Variable		
	Change in Domestic Profit Margin (1)	Change in Foreign Profit Margin (2)	Change in Log of Domestic Sales (3)
Change in average effective foreign tax rate	0.039*** (0.018)	−0.056** (0.028)	0.239 (0.180)
Parent R&D/sales 2004	−1.02*** (0.28)	0.180 (0.432)	1.97 (2.80)
Parent advertising/sales 2004	−0.068 (0.120)	0.017 (0.185)	−0.101 (1.20)
Incorporation after 1980	−0.000 (0.008)	0.013 (0.013)	−0.012 (0.082)
Size: log of sales 1996	0.010*** (0.003)	−0.0086* (0.0049)	−0.076** (0.031)
Change in worldwide profit margin	0.657*** (0.039)	0.519*** (0.060)	

Notes: Robust standard errors are in parentheses. The number of firms is $N = 622$. The sample includes companies with worldwide losses in 1996 or 2004. The only requirement is that they report foreign and domestic sales so that profit margins can be computed, which explains the decrease to 622 companies from the original sample of 754. Only nonfinancial parent companies are included.

45

Table 3
The Importance of Intangible Assets

Independent Variables	Dependent Variables			
	Change in Domestic Profit Margin (1)	Change in Foreign Profit Margin (2)	Change in Domestic Profit Margin (3)	Change in Foreign Profit Margin (4)
Parent R&D/sales	−0.676*	0.367	−1.10***	0.223
	(0.365)	(0.514)	(0.28)	(0.429)
Parent advertising/sales	−0.152	0.029	−0.068	0.017
	(0.132)	(0.186)	(0.118)	(0.184)
Incorporation since 1980	−0.007	0.0142	0.000	0.0146
	(0.011)	(0.0153)	(0.008)	(0.0126)
Size: log of sales 1996	0.0169***	−0.0154***	0.010***	−0.0093
	(0.0039)	(0.0056)	(0.003)	(0.0048)
Change in worldwide profit margin	0.742***	0.533***	0.663***	0.507***
	(0.063)	(0.089)	(0.039)	(0.060)
Change in average effective foreign tax rate	0.054	−0.027	0.019	−0.009
	(0.035)	(0.050)	(0.020)	(0.032)
Change in average effective foreign tax rate * R&D/sales	2.48	−4.91**	2.79**	−4.87***
	(1.57)	(2.22)	(1.29)	(1.69)

Notes: Robust standard errors in parentheses. Regressions 1 and 2 are based on the sample of 415 companies that had positive worldwide income in both 1996 and 2004. Regressions 3 and 4 are based on the larger sample of 622 companies.

Table 4

Did Sensitivity to Tax Differentials Increase?

Independent Variables	Change in Foreign Share (1)	Change in Domestic Profit Margin (2)	Change in Foreign Profit Margin (3)	Change in Foreign Share of Sales (4)	Change in Log of Domestic Sales (5)	Change in Log of Foreign Sales (6)
			Dependent Variables			
R&D/sales 2004	0.383 (1.28)	−0.742** (0.359)	0.161 (0.383)	0.374 (0.613)	4.83* (2.83)	2.59 (5.29)
Advertising/sales 2004	−1.46** (0.70)	−0.171 (0.132)	0.006 (0.211)	−0.374* (0.224)	−0.218 (1.03)	−2.12 (1.93)
Incorporation after 1980	−0.112** (0.051)	−0.0072 (0.0109)	0.016 (0.015)	0.0022 (0.0184)	0.045 (0.085)	0.034 (0.159)
Size: log of sales 1996	−0.074*** (0.019)	0.0171*** (0.0039)	−0.0150*** (0.0056)	−0.0144** (0.0061)	−0.051 (0.031)	−0.110* (0.058)
Change in worldwide profit margin		0.762*** (0.063)	0.532*** (0.090)			
Change in average effective foreign tax rate	−0.704*** (0.188)	0.142*** (0.040)	−0.101* (0.057)	−0.181*** (0.067)	0.173 (0.311)	−0.267 (0.582)
Average effective foreign tax rate 1996	−0.546** (0.237)	0.1019** (0.0506)	−0.016 (0.072)	−0.198** (0.086)	−0.109 (0.395)	−1.35* (0.739)

Notes: Robust standard errors are in parentheses. The number of observations is $N = 415$.

47

Table 5

Foreign Share of Income and Profit Margins in 2004

Independent Variables	Dependent Variables				
	Foreign Share of Worldwide Income (1)	Domestic Profit Margin on Sales (2)	Foreign Profit Margin on Sales (3)	Domestic Profit Margin on Sales (4)	Foreign Profit Margin on Sales (5)
Parent R&D/sales	2.45* (1.28)	−0.252 (0.216)	−0.734** (0.368)	−1.36*** (0.387)	0.992 (0.662)
Parent advertising/sales	0.059 (0.233)	0.465*** (0.117)	−0.420** (0.172)	0.493*** (0.116)	−0.464** (0.199)
Incorporation after 1980	−0.089* (0.052)	0.0041 (0.0085)	0.0080 (0.0145)	0.0039 (0.0084)	0.0083 (0.0143)
Size-log of 1996 sales	−0.0192 (0.0188)	0.0045 (0.0031)	−0.0007 (0.0053)	0.0051* (0.0031)	−0.0015 (0.0053)
Average effective foreign tax rate in 2004	−0.914*** (0.188)	0.093*** (0.031)	−0.127** (0.053)	0.023 (0.037)	−0.018 (0.063)
Worldwide profit margin		0.614*** (0.053)	1.25*** (0.091)	0.622*** (0.052)	1.24*** (0.090)
Average effective foreign tax rate * R&D/sales				5.92*** (1.73)	−9.23*** (2.96)

Notes: Robust standard errors are in parentheses. The profit margins on sales variables refer to the ratio of profits to sales.

Table 6

Worldwide Income Growth and the Foreign Share in 1996

Independent Variables	Dependent Variable		
	Growth of Income 1996–2004 (1)	Growth of Income 1996–2004 (2)	Growth of Income 1996–2004 (3)
Foreign share of income 1996	1.35***	1.35***	1.34***
	(0.182)	(0.183)	(0.183)
R&D/sales 2004	8.41	8.55	8.06
	(5.80)	(5.81)	(5.85)
Advertising/sales 2004	−0.680	−0.673	−0.584
	(2.13)	(2.13)	(2.13)
Incorporation after 1980	0.274	0.267	0.271
	(0.175)	(0.176)	(0.176)
Size: log of worldwide sales 1996	−0.084	−0.086	−0.088
	(0.065)	(0.065)	(0.066)
Average effective foreign tax rate 1996		−0.318	−0.748
		(0.594)	(0.820)
Change in average foreign tax rate 1996–2004			0.491
			(0.644)

Notes: Robust standard errors are in parentheses. The number of observations is $N = 415$. The growth in income is the ratio of worldwide income in 2004 to worldwide income in 1996.

49

Table 7
Sources of Change in Effective Foreign Tax Rates 1996–2004

Independent Variables	Change in Foreign Effective Tax Rate (1)	Use of Hybrids (2)	Change in Foreign Effective Tax Rate (3)
Use of hybrid entities	−0.0426** (0.0198)		0.0573* (0.033)
Parent R&D/sales 2004	−0.696** (0.341)	4.54*** (1.11)	0.059 (0.386)
Parent advertising/sales 2004	0.272 (0.183)	−0.295 (0.407)	0.308* (0.179)
Incorporation after 1980	0.0096 (0.0135)	0.0324 (0.0337)	0.0130 (0.0133)
Foreign profit margin 1996	−0.101** (0.050)		−0.106** (0.050)
Financial services dummy	−0.0324 (0.0218)	0.0150 (0.0553)	−0.038* (0.020)
Foreign effective tax rate 1996	−0.881*** (0.0456)	−0.0679 (0.1135)	−0.812*** (0.057)
Foreign share of income 1996		0.103*** (0.035)	
Size: log of sales 1996	0.0006 (0.0054)	0.0429*** (0.0137)	
Hybrid * effective foreign tax rate 1996			−0.264** (0.114)
Hybrid * R&D/Sales			−3.72*** (0.95)

Notes: Robust standard errors are in parentheses. The number of observations is $N = 415$. The hybrid entity variable indicates the extent of the company's use of hybrid entities under the check-the-box rules introduced in 1997. Hybrid * Tax is the interaction of the hybrid variable with the average foreign tax rate in 1996. Hybrid * R&D is the interaction of the hybrid variable with company R&D intensity. The Financial Services dummy variable indicates whether the parent received financial services income from abroad in 1996.

Table B1
Descriptive Statistics

	Sample Mean	Standard Deviation
Average effective foreign tax rate 1996 (%)	21.26	
Average effective foreign tax rate 2004 (%)	15.86	
Foreign share of income 1996	0.381	
Foreign share of income 2004	0.494	
Growth of worldwide profits 2004/1996	2.00	1.71
R&D/sales 2004	0.0146	0.0183
Advertising/sales 2004	0.0180	0.0335
Foreign sales share 1996	0.268	0.207
Foreign sales share 2004	0.321	0.217
Use of hybrids	0.255	0.319
Financial services dummy variable	0.104	0.305
Size 1996 — log of worldwide sales	21.90	1.26
Incorporation after 1980	0.301	0.459
Domestic profit margin 1996	0.0775	0.0940
Domestic profit margin 2004	0.0457	0.0908
Foreign profit margin 1996	0.0579	0.1210
Foreign profit margin 2004	0.1140	0.1614

Notes: Average effective foreign tax rates are the aggregate (i.e., weighted) tax rates based on the entire matched nonfinancial sample. The foreign shares of income are based on aggregates for the nonfinancial sample, which excludes companies with worldwide losses in either 1996 or 2004. That is the sample used in the Table 1 regressions. The remaining data are unweighted means and standard deviations for the same group of companies.